IN ASSOCIATION WITH SQA

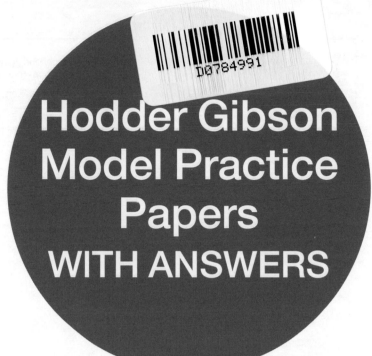

Hodder Gibson
Model Practice
Papers
WITH ANSWERS

PLUS: Official SQA Specimen Paper & 2014 Past Paper With Answers

National 5
Business
Management

2013 Specimen Question Paper,
Model Papers & 2014 Exam

Hodder Gibson Study Skills Advice – General — page 3
Hodder Gibson Study Skills Advice –
   National 5 Business Management — page 5
2013 SPECIMEN QUESTION PAPER — page 7
MODEL PAPER 1 — page 15
MODEL PAPER 2 — page 21
MODEL PAPER 3 — page 27
MODEL PAPER 4 — page 33
2014 EXAM — page 39
ANSWER SECTION — page 47

HODDER
GIBSON
AN HACHETTE UK COMPANY

This book contains the official 2013 SQA Specimen Question Paper and 2014 Exam for National 5 Business Management, with associated SQA approved answers modified from the official marking instructions that accompany the paper.

In addition the book contains model practice papers, together with answers, plus study skills advice. These papers, some of which may include a limited number of previously published SQA questions, have been specially commissioned by Hodder Gibson, and have been written by experienced senior teachers and examiners in line with the new National 5 syllabus and assessment outlines, Spring 2013. This is not SQA material but has been devised to provide further practice for National 5 examinations in 2014 and beyond.

Hodder Gibson is grateful to the copyright holders, as credited on the final page of the book, for permission to use their material.
Every effort has been made to trace the copyright holders and to obtain their permission for the use of copyright material. Hodder Gibson will be happy to receive information allowing us to rectify any error or omission in future editions.

Hachette UK's policy is to use papers that are natural, renewable and recyclable products and made from wood grown in sustainable forests. The logging and manufacturing processes are expected to conform to the environmental regulations of the country of origin.

Orders: please contact Bookpoint Ltd, 130 Park Drive, Abingdon, Oxon OX14 4SE. Telephone: (44) 01235 827720. Fax: (44) 01235 400454. Lines are open 9.00–5.00, Monday to Saturday, with a 24-hour message answering service. Visit our website at www.hoddereducation.co.uk. Hodder Gibson can be contacted direct on: Tel: 0141 848 1609; Fax: 0141 889 6315; email: hoddergibson@hodder.co.uk

This collection first published in 2014 by
Hodder Gibson, an imprint of Hodder Education,
An Hachette UK Company
2a Christie Street
Paisley PA1 1NB

BrightRED   Hodder Gibson is grateful to Bright Red Publishing Ltd for collaborative work in preparation of this book and all SQA Past Paper,
PUBLISHING   National 5 and Higher for CfE Model Paper titles 2014.

Typeset by PDQ Digital Media Solutions Ltd, Bungay, Suffolk NR35 1BY

Printed in the UK

A catalogue record for this title is available from the British Library

ISBN: 978-1-4718-3696-1

3 2 1

2015 2014

Introduction

Study Skills – what you need to know to pass exams!

Pause for thought

Many students might skip quickly through a page like this. After all, we all know how to revise. Do you really though?

Think about this:

"IF YOU ALWAYS DO WHAT YOU ALWAYS DO, YOU WILL ALWAYS GET WHAT YOU HAVE ALWAYS GOT."

Do you like the grades you get? Do you want to do better? If you get full marks in your assessment, then that's great! Change nothing! This section is just to help you get that little bit better than you already are.

There are two main parts to the advice on offer here. The first part highlights fairly obvious things but which are also very important. The second part makes suggestions about revision that you might not have thought about but which WILL help you.

Part 1

DOH! It's so obvious but …

Start revising in good time

Don't leave it until the last minute – this will make you panic.

Make a revision timetable that sets out work time AND play time.

Sleep and eat!

Obvious really, and very helpful. Avoid arguments or stressful things too – even games that wind you up. You need to be fit, awake and focused!

Know your place!

Make sure you know exactly **WHEN and WHERE** your exams are.

Know your enemy!

Make sure you know what to expect in the exam.

How is the paper structured?

How much time is there for each question?

What types of question are involved?

Which topics seem to come up time and time again?

Which topics are your strongest and which are your weakest?

Are all topics compulsory or are there choices?

Learn by DOING!

There is no substitute for past papers and practice papers – they are simply essential! Tackling this collection of papers and answers is exactly the right thing to be doing as your exams approach.

Part 2

People learn in different ways. Some like low light, some bright. Some like early morning, some like evening / night. Some prefer warm, some prefer cold. But everyone uses their BRAIN and the brain works when it is active. Passive learning – sitting gazing at notes – is the most INEFFICIENT way to learn anything. Below you will find tips and ideas for making your revision more effective and maybe even more enjoyable. What follows gets your brain active, and active learning works!

Activity 1 – Stop and review

Step 1

When you have done no more than 5 minutes of revision reading STOP!

Step 2

Write a heading in your own words which sums up the topic you have been revising.

Step 3

Write a summary of what you have revised in no more than two sentences. Don't fool yourself by saying, "I know it, but I cannot put it into words". That just means you don't know it well enough. If you cannot write your summary, revise that section again, knowing that you must write a summary at the end of it. Many of you will have notebooks full of blue/black ink writing. Many of the pages will not be especially attractive or memorable so try to liven them up a bit with colour as you are reviewing and rewriting. **This is a great memory aid, and memory is the most important thing.**

Activity 2 — Use technology!

Why should everything be written down? Have you thought about "mental" maps, diagrams, cartoons and colour to help you learn? And rather than write down notes, why not record your revision material?

What about having a text message revision session with friends? Keep in touch with them to find out how and what they are revising and share ideas and questions.

Why not make a video diary where you tell the camera what you are doing, what you think you have learned and what you still have to do? No one has to see or hear it, but the process of having to organise your thoughts in a formal way to explain something is a very important learning practice.

Be sure to make use of electronic files. You could begin to summarise your class notes. Your typing might be slow, but it will get faster and the typed notes will be easier to read than the scribbles in your class notes. Try to add different fonts and colours to make your work stand out. You can easily Google relevant pictures, cartoons and diagrams which you can copy and paste to make your work more attractive and **MEMORABLE**.

Activity 3 – This is it. Do this and you will know lots!

Step 1

In this task you must be very honest with yourself! Find the SQA syllabus for your subject (www.sqa.org.uk). Look at how it is broken down into main topics called MANDATORY knowledge. That means stuff you MUST know.

Step 2

BEFORE you do ANY revision on this topic, write a list of everything that you already know about the subject. It might be quite a long list but you only need to write it once. It shows you all the information that is already in your long-term memory so you know what parts you do not need to revise!

Step 3

Pick a chapter or section from your book or revision notes. Choose a fairly large section or a whole chapter to get the most out of this activity.

With a buddy, use Skype, Facetime, Twitter or any other communication you have, to play the game "If this is the answer, what is the question?". For example, if you are revising Geography and the answer you provide is "meander", your buddy would have to make up a question like "What is the word that describes a feature of a river where it flows slowly and bends often from side to side?".

Make up 10 "answers" based on the content of the chapter or section you are using. Give this to your buddy to solve while you solve theirs.

Step 4

Construct a wordsearch of at least 10 X 10 squares. You can make it as big as you like but keep it realistic. Work together with a group of friends. Many apps allow you to make wordsearch puzzles online. The words and phrases can go in any direction and phrases can be split. Your puzzle must only contain facts linked to the topic you are revising. Your task is to find 10 bits of information to hide in your puzzle, but you must not repeat information that you used in Step 3. DO NOT show where the words are. Fill up empty squares with random letters. Remember to keep a note of where your answers are hidden but do not show your friends. When you have a complete puzzle, exchange it with a friend to solve each other's puzzle.

Step 5

Now make up 10 questions (not "answers" this time) based on the same chapter used in the previous two tasks. Again, you must find NEW information that you have not yet used. Now it's getting hard to find that new information! Again, give your questions to a friend to answer.

Step 6

As you have been doing the puzzles, your brain has been actively searching for new information. Now write a NEW LIST that contains only the new information you have discovered when doing the puzzles. Your new list is the one to look at repeatedly for short bursts over the next few days. Try to remember more and more of it without looking at it. After a few days, you should be able to add words from your second list to your first list as you increase the information in your long-term memory.

FINALLY! Be inspired...

Make a list of different revision ideas and beside each one write **THINGS I HAVE** tried, **THINGS I WILL** try and **THINGS I MIGHT** try. Don't be scared of trying something new.

And remember – "FAIL TO PREPARE AND PREPARE TO FAIL!"

National 5 Business Management

The course

The National 5 Business Management course should enable you to develop:

- knowledge and understanding of the ways in which society relies on business to satisfy our needs
- an insight into the systems that organisations use to ensure customers' needs are met
- enterprising skills and attributes by providing you with opportunities to explore realistic business situations
- financial awareness through business contexts
- an insight into how organisations organise their resources for maximum efficiency and to improve their overall performance
- an awareness of how external influences impact on organisations.

How the course is graded

The grade you finally get for National 5 Business Management depends on three things:

- the three internal Unit Assessments you do in school or college: "Understanding Business", "Management of People and Finance", and "Management of Marketing and Operations"; these don't count towards the final grade, but you must have passed them before you can get a course award and then a final grade
- your Assignment – this is submitted in April for marking by SQA and counts for 30% of your final grade
- the exam you sit in May – this counts for 70% of your final grade.

General advice

Although National 5 Business Management is a new qualification, it does draw most of its topics and content from the Standard Grade and Intermediate 2 Business Management courses. When studying the National 5 Business Management course and preparing for the external assessment, you should take account of previous advice issued by SQA in the External Assessment Reports prepared by the Principal Assessors for Standard Grade and Intermediate 2 qualifications.

Command words

It is often the case that candidates in the exam misunderstand what the question is asking them as they don't realise the importance of what is called the "Command Word". For example, if a question asks you to **identify** something, you only need to say what it is. However, if the question asks you to **describe** it, then you need to give some of the main features.

Example 1

Question: *Identify a source of finance for a business.*
1 mark

Acceptable answer: *A source of finance could be a Bank Loan.*

This answer will receive a mark as it does what the command word **identify** has asked.

Example 2

Question: *Describe a source of finance for a business.*
1 mark

Acceptable answer: *A loan from a bank which can be repaid with interest, over a period of time.*

In this case, where the command word is **describe**, there would be no marks awarded for the answer given in Example 1. You need to include some features of a bank loan (describe it) in order to get the mark. Remember, it is good practice to always answer in sentences.

So make sure you read the question carefully, checking the command word to see how you need to write your answer.

Context

Section 1 questions in the exam will provide you with a short piece of stimulus material, sometimes called a case study, with information about a small or medium sized business. The questions that follow will mostly relate to the case study and your answers should reflect the context given.

For example, if the case study is about a charity, then your answers should relate to a charity.

Example 3

Question: *Give an objective for the RSPCA.* **1 mark**
Acceptable answer: *To promote animal welfare.*

Because the RSPCA is a charity there are a number of objectives that would not be suitable for them. For example, you would get no marks for saying an objective would be to make as much profit as possible.

Remember to relate all your answers to the business or organisation from the case study.

Marks

Check the number of marks for each question. Too often candidates write too much or too little. If there is only one mark available then you only need to make one point. It might be safer to give two just in case, but only if you have time. If there are four marks available, then you need to make four points to get full marks.

Check to make sure that you have made enough points in your answer to get full marks.

Topic areas

Understanding Business and Marketing are areas where candidates normally do well in exams. However, Finance proves tricky for a lot of students, and, to a lesser extent, so do Human Resources and Operations. There is no way to avoid questions on these topics, so you will need to learn what is contained in each.

Finance

There are only five parts to finance: sources of finance, break-even, cash budgeting, profit statement and technology.

For sources of finance you only need to be aware of where the organisation can get money from. Remember, this can be either to invest in the business or to overcome a cash flow problem, so make sure you understand which you should write about, as the acceptable answers may be different for different questions.

For break-even, you need to memorise the formula for calculating contribution and break-even. Once you have done this, these questions should be fairly straightforward. Don't be put off by the use of numbers. The calculations you may be asked to carry out are relatively simple and you will be able to use a calculator.

When looking at cash budgets in a question, it is always better to read left to right rather than up and down. Look for trends, such as a source of income going down, or a cost that is increasing. These would show potential problems which the business should worry about.

Human resources

Candidates often confuse what is included under each heading for recruitment and selection.

- **Recruitment**

  It is generally accepted that the recruitment stage involves job analysis, job description, person specification, the decision about whether to recruit internally or externally, and, finally, the advertisement of the job.

- **Selection**

  Here you will be expected to give answers about selection methods. These could include application forms/CVs, references, interviews and the various forms of testing available.

Remember that the recruitment stage is about the job and the selection stage is about picking the right person!

Operations

The main problem encountered by candidates is what is meant by quality. There are only two methods you need to know about.

- **Quality control**

  This is a simple system where the quality of raw materials is checked at the start of production, and the quality of the finished product is checked at the end.

- **Quality management**

  Here quality is checked at every stage from carrying out market research to learn what the customers need from the product, to providing quality after-sales service.

Problem answers

Some of the answers you might give to a question are not suitable for gaining marks. Try not to use answers such as "quicker", "easier", "more efficient", "saves time", "saves money" as these do not attract marks. They are *relative terms* and if you do use them you must show what you are comparing them to.

Example 4

Question: *Outline* an advantage of using spreadsheets in Finance. **1 mark**

Acceptable answer: *Formulas in the spreadsheet will carry out calculations automatically.*

You would not get a mark for saying it is faster than doing calculations by hand.

Always use business terminology in your answers – this is far more likely to get you the marks!

Good luck!

A lot of what you will learn in National 5 Business Management is common sense. As a consumer and a member of society you are already aware of most of the course content. The challenge is to make sure you understand the terms used. Hard work and good preparation go a long way, so keep calm and don't panic! GOOD LUCK!

NATIONAL 5

2013 Specimen
Question Paper

National
Qualifications
SPECIMEN ONLY

SQ04/N5/01

Business Management

Date — Not applicable

Duration — 1 hour and 30 minutes

Total marks — 70

SECTION 1 — 30 marks

Attempt BOTH questions.

SECTION 2 — 40 marks

Attempt ALL questions.

Before attempting the questions you must check that your answer booklet is for the same subject and level as this question paper.

Read all questions carefully before attempting.

On the answer booklet, you must clearly identify the question number you are attempting.

Use **blue** or **black** ink.

You may use a calculator.

Before leaving the examination room you must give your answer booklet to the Invigilator. If you do not, you may lose all the marks for this paper.

SECTION 1 — 30 marks

Attempt BOTH questions

> **Palladium Executive Hire**
>
> Asif Ali owns Palladium Executive Hire. The business specialises in renting luxury cars, such as the Rolls Royce Phantom and Bentley, at affordable prices.
>
> Asif received financial support from his family and the Prince's Trust Youth Business Scotland (YBS).
>
> The business has an excellent website; this is just one of the ways in which it offers a "first-class service" to its customers. The website enables the business to advertise promotions and special offers with discounts to customers who book online.
>
>
> Palladium Executive Hire
>
> © 2010 PSYBT
>
> Palladium Executive Hire plans to expand and is currently seeking to recruit new staff. The business offers employees good pay and this has resulted in a highly motivated workforce.
>
> *Adapted from* www.psybt.org.uk/case-study/palladium-executive-hire *(December 2012)*

You should note that although the following questions are based on the case study above, you will need to make use of knowledge and understanding you have gained whilst studying the Course.

1. (a) (i) Give a reason Asif approached YBS for financial support rather than his bank.   **1**

      (ii) Identify 2 areas of support, other than finance, provided by YBS.   **2**

   (b) From the case study, identify two business aims for Palladium Executive Hire.   **2**

   (c) Describe how stakeholders, identified in the case study, may influence Palladium Executive Hire.   **4**

   (d) Asif benefits from a highly motivated workforce.

      Outline ways that Asif could motivate his staff, other than pay.   **2**

   (e) Asif offers a first-class service to his customers.

      Describe ways that the business can ensure it maintains a quality service.   **4**

Total marks   **15**

MARKS

The SSE Hydro: Scotland's New Home of Live Entertainment

The Hydro is located close to Glasgow City Centre and has changed the city's skyline. The building is unusual with a unique exterior wrapped in foil "pillows" which allows the arena to glow at night.

The Hydro is a venue for hire. It is the landlord for event organisers to hire and to host their event.

The arena will seat 12,000 people who will be able to enjoy a host of events, including concerts, arena shows and sports. The cost of attending an event at The Hydro will depend on a number of factors, including the scale of the production and the artists appearing.

The Hydro is located next to the Scottish Exhibition and Conference Centre and is a few minutes' walk from a railway station, which should limit traffic congestion. Being environmentally friendly is a priority for The Hydro. However, it is also next to major road links and this required a 1,600-space car park to be built to accommodate those people travelling by car.

Despite the recession causing tough financial times, a large number of jobs were created. Holding events creates the potential for over £100m to be injected into the local economy each year.

Adapted from www.thehydro.com

You should note that although the following questions are based on the case study above, you will need to make use of knowledge and understanding you have gained whilst studying the Course.

2. (a) State the sector of industry The Hydro operates in.　　1

 (b) Using examples from the case study, describe reasons for The Hydro's choice of location.　　3

 (c) Describe reasons why the event organisers hosting an event in The Hydro would prepare a cash budget to help them make decisions.　　3

 (d) Describe factors that the event organisers hosting an event in The Hydro will consider before setting prices for tickets.　　3

 (e) The case study identifies external factors that may impact on The Hydro.

 Outline 3 ways these external factors may impact on The Hydro.　　3

 (f) The Hydro has created a number of jobs for the local economy.

 Justify a method of selection that The Hydro might use to choose employees.　　2

　　　　　　　　　　　　　　　Total marks　　**15**

MARKS

SECTION 2 — 40 marks

Attempt ALL questions

3. (a) Introduction is the first stage in the product life cycle.

　　　Identify other stages of the product life cycle. **3**

　(b) Describe the advantages of branding to an organisation. **4**

　(c) Compare desk research and field research. **3**

Total marks　10

4. (a) Describe methods of production that could be used by an organisation. **3**

　(b) Outline 3 factors an organisation would consider when choosing a supplier. **3**

　(c) Describe the advantages and disadvantages to an organisation of using automation (capital-intensive). **4**

Total marks　10

5. (a) A charity is an example of an organisation that operates in the third sector.

　　(i) Identify the other sectors of the economy.

　　(ii) Describe each of the sectors identified in (a)(i). **4**

　(b) Explain the importance of good customer service. **2**

　(c) Describe the advantages and disadvantages of setting up in business as a sole trader. **4**

Total marks　10

MARKS

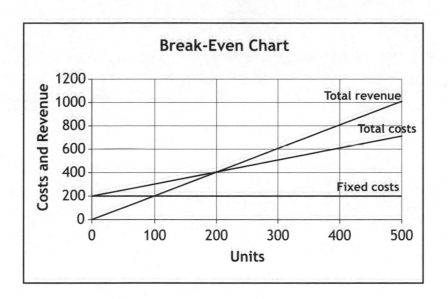

6. (a) (i) From the break-even chart, identify:
- the number of units sold at break-even point
- total revenue at break-even point. **2**

   (ii) Calculate the selling price per unit. **1**

   (iii) Define the term "fixed costs" and give an example of a fixed cost. **2**

(b) The finance department of an organisation will use ICT.

   Justify the use of a spreadsheet to prepare financial information. **3**

(c) Define the following terms found in a profit statement:
- gross profit
- net profit. **2**

Total marks 10

[END OF SPECIMEN QUESTION PAPER]

Model Paper 1

Whilst this Model Practice Paper has been specially commissioned by Hodder Gibson for use as practice for the National 5 exams, the key reference documents remain the SQA Specimen Paper 2013 and the SQA Past Paper 2014.

HODDER
GIBSON
LEARN MORE

National Qualifications
MODEL PAPER 1

Business Management

Duration — 1 hour and 30 minutes

Total marks — 70

SECTION 1 — 30 marks

Attempt BOTH questions.

SECTION 2 — 40 marks

Attempt ALL questions.

Before attempting the questions you must check that your answer booklet is for the same subject and level as this question paper.

Read all questions carefully before attempting.

On the answer booklet, you must clearly identify the question number you are attempting.

Use **blue** or **black** ink.

You may use a calculator.

Before leaving the examination room you must give your answer booklet to the Invigilator.
If you do not, you may lose all the marks for this paper.

MARKS

SECTION 1 – 30 marks

Attempt BOTH questions

Roadwise Driver Training

Roadwise Driver Training, based in Aberdeen, is the largest independent driver training provider in the North East of Scotland.

Roadwise Driver Training was established in 1994 by founding manager Dave Watson, a former Police Class 1 Driver and Driving Instructor. Along with former business partner and police colleague, Roddie Munro, he developed Roadwise. It is now a leader in the field of driver training in the UK.

Roadwise is not only at the cutting edge of driver training but also broke new ground by becoming the first social enterprise driver training provider. Profit generated by Roadwise directly supports the work of Aberdeen Foyer who work to prevent and reduce youth homelessness and unemployment in Aberdeen and Aberdeenshire.

Safety is imbedded in every aspect of Roadwise from driving lessons or Under 17 tuition for learner drivers to skid training, defensive driving and road familiarisation as part of corporate packages tailor-made for companies.

Source – roadwisedrivertraining.co.uk

You should note that although the following questions are based on the case study above, you will need to make use of knowledge and understanding you have gained whilst studying the Course.

1. (a)   (i) From the case study, identify the market segments Roadwise targets.   2

    (ii) Outline the benefits of having different products for different customers.   3

    (b) Describe the costs and benefits of off the job training for an organisation.   4

    (c) Outline the benefits of Roadwise having a website for its business.   4

    (d)   (i) From the case study, identify the sector of industry that Roadwise operates in.   1

    (ii) Describe the sector identified in (d) (i).   1

                                                        Total marks   **15**

MARKS

Angus Soft Fruits Ltd is one of the leading suppliers of strawberries, raspberries, blueberries and blackberries to UK retailers. The business was established in 1994 with the objective of benefiting both customers and growers through direct contact between the two.

Angus Soft Fruits Ltd has a strict ethical policy which sets out minimum standards expected of grower-suppliers. The business takes its responsibility to the natural environment very seriously. It undertakes regular audits of its grower-suppliers to ensure that they are achieving and in the majority of cases exceeding industry standards.

It controls every aspect of the supply chain from propagation of plants to delivery to our customers' depots to ensure consumer quality expectations are exceeded. To achieve this it employs a team of specialists with detailed product knowledge.

You should note that although the following questions are based on the case study above, you will need to make use of knowledge and understanding you have gained whilst studying the Course.

2. (a) Outline the benefits to Angus Soft Fruits Ltd of having a strict ethical policy.   3

    (b) (i) From the case study identify methods Angus Soft Fruits uses to ensure quality.   2

         (ii) Describe the benefits for Angus Soft Fruits in providing quality products.   2

    (c) Angus Soft Fruits Ltd employ a team of specialists to help achieve its aims.

         Describe steps involved in the recruitment process.   3

    (d) (i) From the case study, identify the type of organisation that Angus Soft Fruits operates.   1

         (ii) Give 3 features of this type of business.   2

    (e) Identify sources of finance for Angus Soft Fruits.   2

                                                    Total marks   15

MARKS

SECTION 2 — 40 marks

Attempt ALL questions

3. (a) Describe the benefits of using a bank loan for an organisation. 2

   (b) State 2 fixed costs for an organisation. 2

   (c) Using the following information, calculate the Net Profit of the business. 2

Sales	£280,000
Production costs	£120,000
Other expenses	£85,000

   (d) Justify the use of cash budgets for an organisation. 4

   Total marks 10

4. (a) Outline methods a business could use when selecting new employees. 2

   (b) Compare 2 types of payment systems used by organisations. 2

   (c) Identify 3 areas of discrimination that are not allowed under the Equality Act 2010. 3

   (d) Describe the employers' responsibilities under the Health and Safety at Work Act. 3

   Total marks 10

5. (a) Outline the stages of the product life cycle. 4

   (b) Describe methods of field research, which could be used by an organisation. 4

   (c) Identify 2 considerations an organisation should make when launching a new product. 2

   Total marks 10

6. (a) Explain why batch production would be the most suitable for an organisation such as Baxter's. 2

   (b) Compare quality control with quality management. 2

   (c) Outline the benefits of using modern technology in the manufacturing process. 3

   (d) Outline the factors that an organisation should consider before choosing a supplier. 3

   Total marks 10

[END OF MODEL PRACTICE PAPER]

Model Paper 2

Whilst this Model Practice Paper has been specially commissioned by Hodder Gibson for use as practice for the National 5 exams, the key reference documents remain the SQA Specimen Paper 2013 and the SQA Past Paper 2014.

National Qualifications
MODEL PAPER 2

Business Management

Duration — 1 hour and 30 minutes

Total marks — 70

SECTION 1 — 30 marks

Attempt BOTH questions.

SECTION 2 — 40 marks

Attempt ALL questions.

Before attempting the questions you must check that your answer booklet is for the same subject and level as this question paper.

Read all questions carefully before attempting.

On the answer booklet, you must clearly identify the question number you are attempting.

Use **blue** or **black** ink.

You may use a calculator.

Before leaving the examination room you must give your answer booklet to the Invigilator. If you do not, you may lose all the marks for this paper.

MARKS

SECTION 1 — 30 marks

Attempt BOTH questions

Xtreme Business Solutions

Xtreme Business Solutions was established in 2003 to supply voice and data cabling services to the rapidly expanding IT marketplace in Scotland. Today XBS has established itself as one the leading suppliers of Structured Network Cabling and associated IT solutions in the UK.

Xtreme Business Solutions provides a comprehensive range of IT solutions to meet each client's individual requirements. XBS also believes in building long-term working relationships with both its clients and suppliers.

Focussed on high quality working practices, it invests heavily in knowledgeable and qualified technical people. This ensures that projects are handled in a professional manner and that the finished product meets or exceeds current industry standards.

XBS prides itself on its astute market awareness ensuring that it is always at the leading edge.

Source – www.extremesolutionsltd.com

You should note that although the following questions are based on the case study above, you will need to make use of knowledge and understanding you have gained whilst studying the Course.

1. (a) (i) From the case study, outline ways XBS try to ensure customer satisfaction. 2

    (ii) Justify the importance of customer satisfaction to an organisation. 3

   (b) Outline how the use of modern technology could improve marketing within an organisation. 3

   (c) (i) From the case study, identify the type of production that XBS would use. 1

    (ii) Describe the benefits of this type of production. 3

   (d) Describe internal factors that XBS should take into account when taking on a new contract. 3

   Total marks 15

MARKS

Concerns have grown as part of the Aberdeenshire coast has been left without inshore rescue cover as a result of the closure of the local charity Maritime Rescue Institute (MRI). The MRI announced in February it was being forced to close its doors after failing to recover from storm damage. The institute said it was left without any boats in the water after its base at the harbour was deluged in the storm and floods of December 2012.

The charity said it had already been struggling with falling donations partly due to the recession, and a reduction in government support. Its board decided there was no other option but to close down. Its withdrawal left the Kincardineshire coast being covered only by voluntary lifeboats at Aberdeen and Montrose.

A business case was being put together by another charity to replace the inshore rescue service as a matter of urgency. Stonehaven is now hoping to get an inshore lifeboat in July and volunteers are being sought.

Source – www.bbc.co.uk/news

You should note that although the following questions are based on the case study above, you will need to make use of knowledge and understanding you have gained whilst studying the Course.

2. (a) MRI found it was struggling with falling donations.

    Identify 3 other sources of finance for a charity.   3

    (b) The other charity is now looking for volunteers for the lifeboat service.

    Outline methods of selection an organisation could use to ensure they pick the right staff.   3

    (c) From the case study, identify external factors affecting MRI.   3

    (d) Compare charities with private limited companies in terms of:

    • ownership

    • control

    • finance.   3

    (e) Describe the influence of stakeholders, identified from the case study, on charities.   3

                                                                          Total marks   15

MARKS

SECTION 2 — 40 marks
Attempt ALL questions

3. (a) Describe elements in the marketing mix. 4

   (b) Outline the possible drawbacks of developing a brand name. 3

   (c) Discuss the use of road transport for the physical distribution of products to market. 3

   Total marks 10

4. (a) Outline the problems for an organisation of under-stocking. 4

   (b) Describe 3 methods a manufacturer could use to ensure they produce a quality product. 3

   (c) Discuss the importance of avoiding wastage in production for an organisation. 3

   Total marks 10

5. (a) Outline what is contained in a person specification. 2

   (b) Describe 2 types of payment systems used by organisations. 2

   (c) Explain the benefits to an organisation of providing good pay and conditions for its employees. 3

   (d) Induction training is given to new employees of an organisation.

   Describe other methods of training that existing employees might receive. 3

   Total marks 10

6. (a) Describe measures an organisation can take when faced with a negative closing balance in their cash budget. 3

   (b) Distinguish between the following terms:

   (i) gross profit and net profit

   (ii) fixed costs and variable costs. 2

   (c) Give 2 examples of variable costs. 2

   (d) Describe how an organisation may use spreadsheets. 3

   Total marks 10

[END OF MODEL PRACTICE PAPER]

Model Paper 3

Whilst this Model Practice Paper has been specially commissioned by Hodder Gibson for use as practice for the National 5 exams, the key reference documents remain the SQA Specimen Paper 2013 and the SQA Past Paper 2014.

National Qualifications
MODEL PAPER 3

Business Management

Duration — 1 hour and 30 minutes

Total marks — 70

SECTION 1 — 30 marks
Attempt BOTH questions.

SECTION 2 — 40 marks
Attempt ALL questions.

Before attempting the questions you must check that your answer booklet is for the same subject and level as this question paper.

Read all questions carefully before attempting.

On the answer booklet, you must clearly identify the question number you are attempting.

Use **blue** or **black** ink.

You may use a calculator.

Before leaving the examination room you must give your answer booklet to the Invigilator.
If you do not, you may lose all the marks for this paper.

MARKS

SECTION 1 — 30 marks

Attempt BOTH questions

The Chocolate Tree

It all began over a cup of thick hot chocolate in Barcelona. The idea for The Chocolate Tree was to build a travelling chocolaterie which would tour the British music festivals. As well as this method of selling, it has a shop based in Edinburgh and also sells via its website.

All of the products are hand crafted by a small team, working closely together to create small batches of the highest quality. The team are always experimenting with new ideas and sourcing the best ingredients. Where possible these are always local or organic.

The Chocolate Tree is proud to be one of the first UK chocolatiers to not only work with chocolate, but make chocolate from beans. It hopes to work more directly with farmers of cacao and have much more control over the quality of the chocolate it produces.

Adapted from www.the-chocolate-tree.co.uk

You should note that although the following questions are based on the case study above, you will need to make use of knowledge and understanding you have gained whilst studying the Course.

1. (a) (i) The Chocolate Tree is an entrepreneurial business.

            State the meaning of the word "entrepreneur".   1

        (ii) State 2 business objectives of The Chocolate Tree.   2

    (b) The Chocolate Tree has employees who work in a specialised area.

         Describe the process that The Chocolate Tree may use when recruiting new staff.   4

    (c) Identify 2 methods of training that may be suitable for The Chocolate Tree to use for its employees.   2

    (d) The Chocolate Tree tries to work more directly with farmers who provide its raw materials.

         Explain how this could be said to demonstrate an ethical approach to business.   2

    (e) The Chocolate Tree works with farmers to gain control over the quality of the chocolate it produces.

         Describe a system of quality management than an organisation may use to ensure it produces high quality products.   4

                                                              Total marks   **15**

MARKS

TRAID

TRAID (Textile Recycling for Aid and International Development) is a charity which was set up in 1999.

It is based in London and works to recycle and re-use Britain's unwanted clothes and shoes. It stops clothes from going to landfill sites by providing textile recycling banks. The money raised supports many different types of projects.

TRAID operates more than 1500 textile recycling banks across the UK. Clothing donated to TRAID recycling banks is transported to a central warehouse and sorted by hand according to quality and style. The clothing is then sold back to the public in one of TRAID's charity shops in London or via the website. Damaged clothes which can't be resold in TRAID'S shops are remade and redesigned into new one-off pieces and sold under the award-winning recycled fashion label, TRAIDremade.

The money that is raised is used to expand TRAID's recycling activities and is also donated to overseas development projects which focus on projects to improve environmental and social conditions in the textile supply and production chain.

You should note that although the following questions are based on the case study above, you will need to make use of knowledge and understanding you have gained whilst studying the Course.

2. (a)   (i)   State the main aim of a charity such as TRAID.   1

        (ii)   Outline reasons for TRAID operating in London and online.   3

   (b)   Outline 2 marketing methods that TRAID might use, apart from using its website.   2

   (c)   Identify 3 costs that TRAID may have to pay to operate its business.   3

   (d)   Identify 2 sources of finance that may be available to TRAID if it wishes to open a new shop.   2

   (e)   TRAID uses labour intensive methods to sort clothes in its central warehouse.

       Describe advantages and disadvantages of this system.   4

Total marks   15

MARKS

SECTION 2 — 40 marks
Attempt ALL questions

3. (a) Describe methods used by an organisation when developing a new product.   4

   (b) Discuss the importance of ethical marketing in modern business.   3

   (c) Outline 3 methods of promotion used in business.   3

   Total marks   10

4. (a) Outline the importance of quality management in maintaining the good reputation of an organisation.   3

   (b) Describe the benefits of recycling to an organisation.   2

   (c) Outline the problems associated with over-stocking and under-stocking.   4

   (d) Justify the use of computer technology in controlling stock.   1

   Total marks   10

5. (a) Describe 3 external factors.   3

   (b) Explain the importance of customer satisfaction to an organisation.   3

   (c) Describe 2 internal factors.   2

   (d) Describe the interest in and influence of shareholders on an organisation.   2

   Total marks   10

6. (a) (i) Identify 2 ways of advertising for new staff.   2

      (ii) Outline an advantage and a disadvantage of one of the methods identified in (a) (i).   2

   (b) Discuss the role of trade unions.   4

   (c) Justify the use of a "safe working practices" policy used by an organisation to ensure the safety of its employees.   2

   Total marks   10

[END OF MODEL PRACTICE PAPER]

Model Paper 4

Whilst this Model Practice Paper has been specially commissioned by Hodder Gibson for use as practice for the National 5 exams, the key reference documents remain the SQA Specimen Paper 2013 and the SQA Past Paper 2014.

National
Qualifications
MODEL PAPER 4

Business Management

Duration — 1 hour and 30 minutes

Total marks — 70

SECTION 1 — 30 marks

Attempt BOTH questions.

SECTION 2 — 40 marks

Attempt ALL questions.

Before attempting the questions you must check that your answer booklet is for the same subject and level as this question paper.

Read all questions carefully before attempting.

On the answer booklet, you must clearly identify the question number you are attempting.

Use **blue** or **black** ink.

You may use a calculator.

Before leaving the examination room you must give your answer booklet to the Invigilator.
If you do not, you may lose all the marks for this paper.

MARKS

SECTION 1 — 30 marks

Attempt BOTH questions

Just Dogs

Just Dogs was established in December 2006 by Gemma Johnstone. As a devoted dog owner and dog lover Gemma wanted to offer "doggy" people the chance to visit a shop that would offer a great selection of quality and unique dog

accessories and supplies. Whilst the online doggy market proves popular, Gemma wanted to give dog owners the opportunity to be able to visit the shop, see the products and try them out before purchasing. Gemma also likes to be on hand to offer advice and tips to customers who visit the shop which is based in Edinburgh

Gemma is currently studying towards the Advanced Diploma in Canine Behaviour. This means that she is able to provide competent advice regarding dog training, behaviour and nutrition. It is important to Gemma to be able to offer a personal, tailored service to customers and this is central to the way the business is operated.

Just Dogs promotes responsible dog ownership. All of its practical doggy products are accompanied with useful guidance, tips and messages. This allows owners to look after their dogs in the best possible manner.

Adapted from www.justdogsshop.co.uk

You should note that although the following questions are based on the case study above, you will need to make use of knowledge and understanding you have gained whilst studying the Course.

1. (a) (i) From the case study, identify the type of business that Gemma operates.   1

      (ii) Using information from the case study and knowledge that you have gained, give 2 examples of good customer service.   2

  (b) Describe 2 costs and 2 benefits to Gemma of operating a website as well as her shop.   4

  (c) Outline methods of promotion that Gemma could use for her business.   3

  (d) Gemma is undertaking training to help her provide a better service to her customers.

     Describe the benefits of staff training.   3

  (e) Describe 2 costs that Gemma may have in her business.   2

Total marks   15

MARKS

> ### Tree of Knowledge
>
> Tree of Knowledge (TOK) is a company that was set up to provide new services to support learning for children and adults. TOK's aim is to help them become more enterprising in both their education and personal development.
>
>
>
> TOK provides goods and services for both schools and businesses to help improve motivation. It wants to "put fun back into schools and workplaces all over the UK".
>
> Directors of TOK appeared on the popular BBC2 show, Dragons' Den, asking the dragons for £100,000 in return for a 10% share of their business. The main market for TOK products and services is in Scotland, however TOK was looking for investment to help it expand into England.
>
> After more than two hours' filming, the directors failed to clinch a deal. One dragon said he'd be unhappy taking a big chunk of the business in return for his investment. Basically, what the dragon was saying was that TOK would get along fine without his money and without giving up a large share in the firm.
>
> *Adapted from www.treeof.com and SQA Intermediate 1 Business Management Past Paper 2012.*

You should note that although the following questions are based on the case study above, you will need to make use of knowledge and understanding you have gained whilst studying the Course.

2. (a)   (i) From the case study, state one aim of TOK.   1

     (ii) Identify 2 services, other than providing motivation, TOK may provide to schools and businesses.   2

   (b) Describe an advantage and a disadvantage of the source of finance identified in the case study for TOK.   2

   (c) Outline the advantages and disadvantages of having additional partners in a business.   4

   (d) Outline the interests of 3 stakeholders in a business such as TOK.   3

   (e) TOK operates as a limited company.
        Describe the advantages and disadvantages of operating as a limited company.   3

                                                                                                 Total marks   15

MARKS

SECTION 2 — 40 marks

Attempt ALL questions

3. (a) Identify 3 sources of finance that may be available to a partnership. 3

   (b) Discuss the importance of managing cash flow in an organisation. 3

   (c) Identify 2 possible solutions for an organisation with cash flow problems. 2

   (d) Define the following terms:
   - gross profit
   - net profit. 2

   Total marks 10

4. (a) Outline 4 external factors which may affect an organisation. 4

   (b) Explain the importance of the following business objectives:
   - social responsibility
   - profitability
   - survival. 3

   (c) Describe measures an organisation can take to improve its customer service. 3

   Total marks 10

5. (a) List the first 3 stages of the product life cycle. 3

   (b) Describe actions that an organisation may take to revitalise sales of a product that is in decline. 3

   (c) Describe factors that an organisation may consider when setting the price of a new product. 2

   (d) Identify 2 factors that can influence business location. 2

   Total marks 10

6. (a) Describe the impact of industrial action on an organisation. 2

   (b) Explain the benefits to an organisation of employing part-time staff. 3

   (c) Describe the process that an organisation may use to select new employees. 3

   (d) Describe the effect of the Equality Act 2010 on an organisation. 2

   Total marks 10

[END OF MODEL PRACTICE PAPER]

National
Qualifications
2014

X710/75/01

Business Management

MONDAY, 19 MAY

1:00 PM – 2:30 PM

Total marks — 70

SECTION 1 — 30 marks

Attempt BOTH questions

SECTION 2 — 40 marks

Attempt ALL questions

Write your answers clearly in the answer booklet provided. In the answer booklet you must clearly identify the question number you are attempting.

Use **blue** or **black** ink.

You may use a calculator.

Before leaving the examination room you must give your answer booklet to the Invigilator; if you do not, you may lose all the marks for this paper.

MARKS

SECTION 1 — 30 marks

Attempt BOTH questions

It's All Wash and Go for Caroline

Caroline Gray opened Dogs Body Design in Kelso in 2013 with the help of the Prince's Scottish Youth Business Trust (PSYBT). Dogs Body Design provides dog grooming services and sells homemade treats, handmade dog coats and bandanas which are all made locally.

Caroline trained for a year before taking up a post in a dog grooming salon. She then managed a salon before deciding to set up her own business. The PSYBT provided a business advisor who helped her prepare a business plan and cash budget. They also gave a £5000 loan and a grant of £250.

The young entrepreneur's idea proved so successful in just her first couple of weeks that she employed a member of staff. Her popularity means she is fully booked up to a week in advance.

You should note that although the following questions are based on the case study above, you will need to make use of knowledge and understanding you have gained whilst studying the Course.

1. (a) (i) From the case study, identify **2** enterprising skills or qualities that Caroline has demonstrated. 2

     (ii) Outline how these skills or qualities help Caroline develop her business. 2

   (b) From the case study, compare the **2** types of finance provided by the PSYBT. 2

   (c) Caroline provides a service to her customers.

     Justify the importance of providing good customer service. 2

   (d) (i) Caroline employed a member of staff.

     Outline **3** stages in the recruitment process. 3

     (ii) Describe the features of the Equality Act 2010. 2

   (e) (i) From the case study, identify the stage of the product life cycle for Caroline's business. 1

     (ii) Describe the stage identified in (e)(i). 1

Total marks   15

MARKS

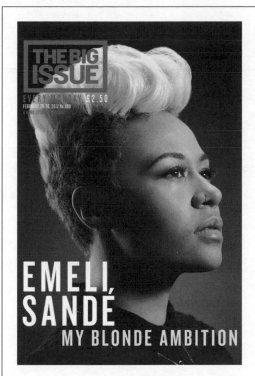

The Big Issue magazine was launched in 1991 by Gordon Roddick and John Bird in response to the problem of homelessness on the streets of London. The Big Issue aims to "help them to help themselves". The partners offer homeless people the opportunity to earn a legitimate income by becoming a vendor and selling magazines on the street. The vendor buys the magazine for £1.25 and sells it for £2.50.

Over twenty years later the organisation has helped thousands of vulnerable people to take control of their lives and currently works with around 2000 homeless people across the UK. The magazine has 63 distribution points nationwide.

The Big Issue is an example of a successful social enterprise. The magazine has clear social benefits and a reputation for getting exciting guest editors and exclusive celebrity contributions which has vastly increased sales.

You should note that although the following questions are based on the case study above, you will need to make use of knowledge and understanding you have gained whilst studying the Course.

2. (a) Compare the objectives of The Big Issue, identified from the case study, with those of a public sector organisation. **2**

(b) (i) From the case study, identify the method of promotion that is used by The Big Issue. **1**

   (ii) Describe other methods of promotion that could be used by The Big Issue. **2**

(c) Explain how external factors could affect the success of The Big Issue. **3**

(d) The Big Issue could use rail to deliver its magazines to its distribution points nationwide.

   (i) Identify another method of distribution. **1**

   (ii) State the advantages and disadvantages of this method. **3**

(e) Describe the factors to be considered when setting the price for The Big Issue. **3**

Total marks **15**

[Turn over

MARKS

SECTION 2 – 40 marks
Attempt ALL questions

3. (a) Discuss the advantages and disadvantages of recycling to an organisation.   **4**

(b) Explain the problems of having too much stock.   **2**

(c) The quality of products is important to all businesses.

   (i) Identify **2** methods of ensuring quality.   **2**

   (ii) Describe the methods identified in (c)(i).   **2**

                      Total marks   **10**

4. (a) Define the following financial terms.
- Fixed Costs
- Variable Costs
- Sales Revenue   **3**

(b) Describe the actions that can be taken by an organisation to reduce costs.   **3**

(c) (i) Justify the use of a spreadsheet in the finance department.   **2**

   (ii) Describe the ways that other software can be used in the finance department.   **2**

                      Total marks   **10**

5. (a) Describe the selection process used to choose the right person for the job.   **4**

(b) (i) Outline **2** methods of industrial action.   **2**

   (ii) Explain the impact of industrial action on an organisation.   **2**

(c) Compare piece-rate with time-rate as methods of calculating wages.   **2**

                      Total marks   **10**

MARKS

6. (a) Outline **2** internal factors that can affect the success of an organisation.

2

(b) Describe factors of production.

3

(c) (i) Identify **2** stakeholders of a supermarket.

2

(ii) Explain how these stakeholders could influence the success of the organisation.

3

Total marks 10

[END OF QUESTION PAPER]

[BLANK PAGE]

SQA AND HODDER GIBSON NATIONAL 5 BUSINESS MANAGEMENT 2014

NATIONAL 5 BUSINESS MANAGEMENT SPECIMEN QUESTION PAPER

General

Questions that ask candidates to *Describe* . . .

Candidates must make a number of relevant, factual points up to the total mark allocation for the question. These should be key points. The points do not need to be in any particular order. Candidates may provide a number of straightforward points or a smaller number of developed points, or a combination of these.

Up to the total mark allocation for this question:
- **1 mark** should be given for each accurate relevant point of knowledge
- **a second mark** could be given for any point that is developed from the point of knowledge

Questions that ask candidates to *Explain* . . .

Candidates must make a number of points that relate cause and effect and/or make the relationships between things clear, for example by showing connections between a process/situation. These should be key reasons and may include theoretical concepts. There is no need to prioritise the reasons. Candidates may provide a number of straightforward reasons or a smaller number of developed reasons, or a combination of these.

Up to the total mark allocation for this question:
- **1 mark** should be given for each accurate relevant point of reason
- **a second mark** could be given for any other point that is developed from the same reason

Section 1

1. (a) (i) Responses could include the following:
- Lower interest rates
- Provide grants that don't need to be paid back
- No need for financial history/credit history
- Age profile
- Longer to pay back

(ii) Responses could include any of the following:
- Help to produce business plans
- Legal advice
- Training courses

(b) Answers must come from the case study given. Identifiable aims are:
- Affordable prices
- First-class service
- Growth/expansion
- Good reputation
- Good employer

(c) Stakeholders used must come from the case study given. Responses could include any of the following:

Asif
- Makes the major decisions and influences the direction of the business

Asif's family
- Have lent money to finance the business and therefore influence the level of investment
- May want to influence decision-making as they have a stake in the business

Customers
- Influence revenues/sales of business by choosing to use the service or not
- Influence reputation of business by their opinions

PSYBT
- Provides finance to allow the business to start up or expand

Employees
- The standard of their work can influence the success of the business
- Can take industrial action which can stop production

Suppliers
- Influence the price of raw materials, which influences the costs of the organisation
- Set the time it will take to deliver the goods which can influence the time the organisation needs to order them
- Can offer discounts to attract organisations to buy more

Candidates are required to consider at least two stakeholders to gain full marks.

(d) Responses could include any of the following:
- Introduce flexible working practices, eg flexi-time
- Improved conditions of service, eg increased holiday entitlement
- Providing training to improve skills
- Identify staff who may have the potential for promotion
- Consult employees on decisions

Candidates are required to consider two methods to gain full marks.

(e) Responses could include any of the following:

Training
- By training workers on customer service, eg how to deal with customer requests or complaints
- By refreshing or updating workers' driving skills, eg putting them on an advanced driving course
- Training will improve the skills of workers and give customers confidence that drivers are up-to-date

Dealing with customers
- Responding to customers' requests more quickly means they may be seen as better than a competitor
- Dealing with customer complaints quickly
- Keeping customers informed on the progress of the complaint and any action being taken

After-sales service
- Following up a hire by asking a customer to give feedback
- Being seen to act on customers' recommendations/opinions

Maintenance of vehicles
- Having vehicles serviced regularly to ensure they are legal and roadworthy
- Ensuring that vehicles are clean and any wear and tear is fixed
- Changing vehicles to newer models to appear more up-to-date

Candidates are required to consider at least two methods to gain full marks.

2. (a) Tertiary sector

(b) Factors to be considered must come from the case study given. Identifiable factors are as follows. Reasons for their choice could include:

Next to existing SECC
- There is existing infrastructure: road, rail links, etc
- Customers are used to going to this area for events so it is familiar to them

Near Glasgow city centre
- There are good public transport links to the venue
- There is hotel accommodation close/next to it for those wishing to stay overnight

Close to railway station
- This allows easy links to the venue for those travelling by rail

Close to main motorway
- This allows easy access to the venue for those driving

Car park opposite
- This allows those driving to park while visiting the venue

Candidates are required to consider at least two factors to gain full marks

(c) Responses could include any of the following:
- To show if an organisation has a surplus of cash
  - This will allow the organisation to look for a way of investing the cash
  - This could also allow them to plan large capital expenditure
- To show if an organisation has a deficit of cash
  - This allows the organisation to take corrective action
- To compare actual figures with forecast figures
  - This will allow an organisation to find ways to control expenditure
- To delegate responsibility to individuals or to departments
- To plan for the future as they have looked at their cash position and can work within it

Candidates are required to consider at least two reasons to gain full marks.

(d) Responses could include any of the following:
- The cost of the artist performing
  - the more famous the artist, the more they may charge for performing
- Price of competitors
  - looking at the cost of other venues will allow the organisation to decide whether or not they want to undercut them
- To create an exclusive image
  - in order to do so, the organisation may need to set a higher price
  - this higher price may give an illusion of quality
- The level of profit the organisation may wish to achieve

- The level of costs they have to cover from the selling price

Candidates are required to consider at least two factors to gain full marks.

(e) Factors to be considered must come from the case study given. Identifiable factors are as follows. Impacts could include:

Economic
- There may be a reduction in consumer spending due to the recession
- There could be an increase in disposable income due to the increase in employment in the area

Environmental
- There could be an increase in complaints from the local community due to the traffic congestion
- There could be complaints due to the increase in pollution from the traffic congestion
- There may be an increase in noise pollution from the arena, meaning constraints are placed on the time they can operate
- There may be an increase in litter which makes the area untidy and unwelcoming for visitors
- Implementing environmentally-friendly measures will increase costs for The Hydro
- Implementing these measures may improve the image of The Hydro

Competition
- Competition with the SECC will have an impact on the number of artists/events that may use The Hydro

Candidates are required to outline the impact of at least two external factors.

(f) Responses could include any of the following:

Interview
- Allows an organisation to assess the candidate's appearance and personality
- Allows them to question the content of the CV or application form
- It also allows a candidate to ask questions

Reference
- Provides key comments on, for example, attendance, attitude, etc
- This allows an organisation to confirm the content of the application form/CV
- Referees might recommend whether the candidate is suitable for the job

Testing
- The organisation can find out the candidate's true personality and not just what they say they are
- They can see how well the candidate copes under pressure
- They can see what decisions the candidate makes in certain conditions (eg handling a difficult customer)

Candidates are required to consider one method of selection only.

Section 2

3. (a) Responses could include any of the following:

- Growth
- Maturity
- Saturation
- Decline

(b) Responses could include any of the following:

- Brands are easily recognised due to the logo
    - this could mean that customers may buy more due to them being familiar
    - this could lead to an increase in the level of profit made
- Brand loyalty can develop
    - this could lead to an increase in market share for the organisation
    - this may make it easier to launch new products
- Marketing/advertising campaigns can be global, with a brand rather than product focus
    - this could save money in the long run as they advertise for all products rather than individual ones
- Customers may be willing to pay more for branded products
    - this could lead to a higher level of profit for the organisation
    - this could also give the product an image of quality
- Branded products can become "trendy"

Candidates are required to consider at least two advantages to gain full marks.

(c) Responses could include any of the following:

- Desk research is the study and evaluation of secondary data, whereas field research involves obtaining first-hand primary data
- Desk research is research that already exists, whereas field research will seek people's opinions directly
- Desk research will be sourced from CD-ROMs, newspapers and websites, whereas field research will be collected through observation, surveys or focus groups
- Desk research can be obtained and analysed relatively quickly, whereas field research can be time-consuming to collect and analyse
- Desk research may have "author bias", whereas field research may have "researcher bias"
- Desk research may be out-of-date, whereas field research is likely to be current
- Desk research collected for one purpose and then used for another may not be relevant, whereas field research can be specific for the purpose it was collected
- Desk research is available to competitors, whereas field research can be kept confidential
- Desk research is relatively inexpensive, whereas the costs of field research may be high

Candidates must demonstrate a true comparison in order to gain any marks. Both sides of the point must be clear but do not need to be linked.

4. (a) Responses could include any of the following:

Job production
- Where a single product is made to a customer's specification
- Product is usually unique/one of a kind
- Labour-intensive method of production

Batch production
- Where similar products are produced in batches at the same time before another batch is started
- Variety of flavours can be produced in batches

Flow production
- Large-scale production where items are produced continuously on production line/in stages
- All products are the same/standardisation
- Capital-intensive production/automation methods used

Candidates are required to consider at least two methods to gain full marks.

(b) Responses could include any of the following:

- Are the suppliers dependable/reliable?
- Are there additional charges for delivering the goods?
- Does the supplier deliver on time?
- Are the supplier's prices competitive?
- Does the supplier give discounts?
- Does the supplier give extended credit?
- Are the goods of an acceptable quality?
- Can the supplier supply the quantity required?

(c) Responses could include any of the following:

Advantages
- Identical products are made
    - This means that the products sold are at the same standard and all customers get the same
    - This could result in less complaints regarding flaws/faults
- Fewer workers are required
    - This would mean a reduction in the wages costs
    - This would reduce overall costs of the organisation
- Machines can operate 24/7
    - This will increase the volume of goods being produced
    - This may allow the organisation to keep up with demand
    - This may allow them to cope at times when there is a rush order

Disadvantages
- Large amounts of machinery and robotics are required
    - This has an impact on the space required to house this
    - This has high initial costs
- Machinery can break down
    - This may cause production to stop completely
    - This may mean customers' orders are not met and they go elsewhere
- Difficult to make products to meet customers' individual requirements

Candidates are required to consider at least one advantage AND one disadvantage to gain full marks.

5. (a) (i) and (ii)
Responses could include any of the following:

Private sector
- Organisations that are owned by private individuals and investors

Public sector
- Organisations that are owned by the government

Candidates must identify and describe two sectors to gain full marks.

(b) Responses could include any of the following:

- Customers will return and thereby not take their custom to a competitor
  - this will result in higher sales and profit being made
- The organisation will receive a good reputation which may attract new customers
  - this could result in a larger market share for the organisation
- Profits may increase due to the increase in trade/customers
  - this may make shareholders happy as they gain higher dividends

(c) Responses could include any of the following:

Advantages
- Owner gets to keep all the profits to themselves
  - this gives the owner a higher return on their investment
- Owner gets to make all the decisions
  - this means there is less argument
  - this also makes decision-making much quicker
- Very easy to set up
  - this is due to very few legal restrictions which may delay the set up
- Customers receive a more personal service
  - this is due to the fact that it's mainly small organisations that set up as sole traders
  - this allows them to know and be closer to their customer

Disadvantages
- Owner has unlimited liability
  - this means the owner runs the risk of losing their personal possessions if the organisation cannot pay its debt
- Finance is limited
  - there may be a limit to how much an individual can invest themselves or have the ability to borrow
- Owner has no one to share workload with
  - this can cause a lot of stress to the owner
  - this may also lead to poor decisions being made
- Owner may have to close the shop when ill or on holiday
  - this may be due to having no other worker in place to run the organisation for them

Candidates are required to consider at least one advantage AND one disadvantage to gain full marks.

6. (a) (i) Number of units at BEP — 200
Total revenue at BEP — £400

(ii) £2 per unit
Eg revenue for 200 units is £400
= £400/200

(iii) Responses could include any of the following:
- Costs that do not vary with the level of production
- Examples may include: rent, rates, salaries

(b) Responses could include any of the following:

- Calculations can be carried out automatically using formulae
  - this saves time once formulae are set up
  - this also eliminates calculation errors if the formulae are set up properly
- Information can be converted into graphs and charts
  - this allows information to be shown in a more appropriate way for some readers
- "If statements" can be used
  - this allows the organisation to calculate potential changes depending on variable that may exist
- Templates can be created
  - this will give a standard layout for staff to use
  - this will give a better corporate image to the documents being produced
- Information can be saved and edited at a later date

Candidates are required to consider at least two justifications to gain full marks.

(c) Responses could include any of the following:

Gross profit
- Profit made from trading (buying and selling) only
- Profit made before other expenses are deducted
- Sales less cost of sales

Net profit
- Final profit made by an organisation
- Profit made after other expenses are deducted
- Gross profit less expenses

Candidate must describe both terms to gain full marks.

NATIONAL 5 BUSINESS MANAGEMENT MODEL PAPER 1

Section 1

1. (a) (i) Market segments must be identified:
- Under 17 tuition
- Learner drivers
- Corporate packages

2

(ii) • Higher level of sales
- More opportunity to achieve profits
- Helps the business grow/survive
- Differentiation of product lines

3

(b) • Employees will be away from the workplace therefore no distractions
- Employees will be more motivated and will be more likely to stay with the organisation
- Off the job training can be expensive so will reduce the profits of the business
- While the employee is away less work will get done meaning lower productivity

4

(c) • Customers can access 24/7
- They can book lessons online
- Can use the website to collect customer information
- Provides advertising for the business
- Will provide contact details for customers

4

(d) (i) Tertiary Sector

1

(ii) The provision of services

1

Total marks 15

2. (a) • They will have a better reputation
- They will attract more customers
- They will attract more sales
- They may be able to charge higher prices

3

(b) (i) Quality measures must be identified from the case study given. Identifiable measures are:
- Quality control
- Quality assurance
- Quality raw materials
- Skilled and motivated employees
- Regular audits

2

(ii) • Fewer customer complaints
- Fewer returns
- Happier customers

2

(c) • Job analysis — to identify the vacancy and establish what the job would entail
- Job description — with details of the tasks involved in the job, responsibilities, pay and conditions etc.
- Person specification — detail the skills, experience and personality required for the job
- Advertise the job — internally or externally

3

(d) (i) Private Limited Company

1

(ii) • Owned by shareholders
- Controlled by a Managing Director and Board of Directors
- They will have limited liability
- It will be easier to attract more finance

2

(e) • Shareholder/investor funds
- Bank loan
- Retained profits

2

Total marks 15

Section 2

3. (a) • Easy to obtain/organise
- Can be paid back in installments
- Can organize to suit cash flow
- Do not lose control of the business

2

(b) • Rent
- Insurance
- Salaries

2

(c)

Sales	£280,000
Production costs	£120,000
Other expenses	£85,000
Gross Profit	*£160,000*
Net Profit	*£75,000*

2

(d) • Can identify times when there will be a cash shortfall
- Can identify when cash will be available to buy fixed assets
- Provides a plan for the future
- Can set targets

4

Total marks 10

4. (a) • Application forms
- Testing
- Interview

2

(b) • Time Rate — paid per hour worked
- Piece Rate — paid for each product made
- Time Rate — doesn't reward those who produce more
- Piece Rate — doesn't reward those who work longer hours

2

(c) • Gender
- Race
- Disability

3

(d) • To ensure safe working environment
- All machinery is well maintained
- Provide adequate training for employees
- Ensure safety for members of the public

3

Total marks 10

5. (a) • Development
• Introduction/Launch
• Growth
• Maturity
• Decline

4

(b) • Observation — watching consumers' behavior
• Interview — 2 way discussion with the consumer
• Telephone survey — phoning consumer at home
• Postal survey — sending questionnaires to the consumer at home

4

(c) • Cost of production
• Competitors prices
• The target market

2

Total marks 10

6. (a) • The same machinery can be used for all varieties of soup — less capital expenditure
• Not enough demand for flow production — saves on waste
• Can vary production to meet market demand

2

(b) • In quality control products are checked at the end of the process whereas they are checked at each stage with quality management.
• There is less waste/scrap with quality assurance than there is with quality control
• Quality management is more expensive to implement than quality control

2

(c) • CAN/Robotics/automation will produce less errors/waste
• More consistent production
• Reduces staff costs

3

(d) • Quality
• Quantity
• Reliability
• Price

3

Total marks 10

NATIONAL 5 BUSINESS MANAGEMENT MODEL PAPER 2

Section 1

1. (a) (i) Ways of ensuring customer satisfaction must come from the case study given. Identifiable methods are:

• Provides a comprehensive range of IT solutions to meet each client's individual requirements
• Building long-term working relationships with both its clients and suppliers
• Investing heavily in knowledgeable and qualified technical people

2

(ii) • Helps maintain the organisation's reputation
• Will bring repeat sales
• Less time spent dealing with complaints

3

(b) • Websites can provide e-commerce
• Text messaging/mobile phones can get immediate feedback from customers
• Broadband allows for immediate updating of information
• Mobile tracking of orders can be offered to customers

3

(c) (i) Job production

1

(ii) • Can be made to customer's exact specification
• Can charge a higher price
• Use skilled workers/specialists

3

(d) • Finance
• Employees
• Current technology

3

Total marks 15

2. (a) • Bank loan
• Government grant
• Merchandise

3

(b) • References
• Interviews
• Testing
• Head hunting/recruitment agencies

3

(c) External factors must come from the case study given. Identifiable factors are:
• Environmental — weather
• Economic — recession
• Political — lack of government support

3

(d) • Charities are owned by their trustees/have no overall owner whereas limited companies are owned by their shareholders
• Charities are controlled by trustees or appointed managers whereas limited companies are controlled by a board of directors
• Charities are largely financed through donations whereas limited companies are financed by shareholders investment

3

(e) • Employees/volunteers can work harder or less hard
• Government can provide grants or withhold them
• Donators/local community can give more or less money

3

Total marks 15

Section 2

3. (a) • Price charged for the product
- Product that is sold to customers
- Place where the product is sold
- Promotion used to inform customers

4

(b) • Expensive to create a brand name
- Brand image can easily be tarnished
- Imitators are hard to stop

3

(c) • Can go door to door
- Less expensive than other methods
- Not suitable for transport to other continents

3

Total marks 10

4. (a) • Loss of sales
- Loss of profits
- Loss of customers
- Damaged reputation

4

(b) • Quality control — check product at end
- Quality management — check at each stage
- Quality inputs — materials, machinery, staff

3

(c) • Waste will increase cost for the business
- The business will then have to deal with the waste ethically
- The reputation of the business may suffer

3

Total marks 10

5. (a) • Abilities/skills required for the job
- Experience needed to do the job
- Personal qualities required of applicants
- Essential and desirable qualities

2

(b) • Piece rate — payment linked to production
- Bonus — additional payment for reaching target
- Time rate — paid per hour at work

2

(c) • Staff will work harder meaning more productive
- Lower staff absences as they are happy at their work
- Lower staff turnover as they are less likely to leave

3

(d) • On the job training where workers are trained while doing the job
- Off the job training where they are trained away from the workplace

3

Total marks 10

6. (a) • They could apply for a bank loan/overdraft
- Seek new shareholders/investors
- Sell off unwanted assets
- Find cheaper supplier
- Economise

3

(b) (i) Gross profit is the profit made on buying and selling stock whereas net profit is the actual profit after all expenses are deducted

(ii) Fixed costs do not change with the level of production whereas variable costs increase the more that is produced

2

(c) • Raw materials
- Packaging
- Production wages

2

(d) • Data can be automatically updated from other sources
- Automatic calculations can be carried out using formulae
- Less chance of human error

3

Total marks 10

NATIONAL 5 BUSINESS MANAGEMENT MODEL PAPER 3

Section 1

1. (a) (i) Someone who successfully combines the factors of production into an original business idea

   1

   (ii) • To produce high quality good
   • To work closely with suppliers/be ethical

   2

   (b) • Identify a vacancy
   • Carry out a job analysis
   • Write a job description
   • Write a person specification
   • Advertise the vacancy

   4

   (c) • Coaching
   • Distance learning
   • Demonstration
   • On the job
   • Off the job

   2

   (d) • The Chocolate Tree is able to control how much it pays for its raw materials to a greater extent rather than working with a middle man
   • The Chocolate Tree can choose only to work with suppliers that meet its business ethics

   2

   (e) • Quality control/TQM
   • Quality assurance
   • Quality circles
   • Benchmarking

   4

   Total marks 15

2. (a) (i) To provide a service and support different types of projects

   1

   (ii) • More opportunities to raise money and support the work of the charity being based in a large city such as London
   • Access to a bigger market having a shop in London
   • Online business gives access to a worldwide market
   • Being online raises the profile of the charity

   3

   (b) • Advertise in the shop window
   • Have a story about its work published in a newspaper to raise its profile
   • Have special offers in its shop and online

   2

   (c) • Rent
   • Electricity
   • Wages
   • Web hosting

   3

   (d) • Bank loan
   • Money from donations

   2

   (e) **Advantages:**
   • Clothes are correctly sorted according to size, colour, condition etc.
   • Not a huge operation so not that many staff are required

Disadvantages:
• May be expensive to operate
• May be a slow process compared to using machinery

4

Total marks 15

Section 2

3. (a) • Desk research
   • Field research
   • Market research
   • Customer testing

   4

   (b) • Creates a "responsible" reputation
   • Attracts consumers by developing trust
   • Promotes a "green" image

   3

   (c) • Television
   • Newspapers
   • Internet
   • Direct mail
   • Outdoor media

   3

   Total marks 10

4. (a) • Customers expect a quality product and may choose a competitor if standards are not met or maintained
   • Poor quality may damage the reputation of the business
   • Poor quality in just one product may lead to poor image for all the organisation's products

   3

   (b) • May provide an additional income
   • Promotes the organisation in a good light to its customers
   • Reduces wastage

   2

   (c) **Over stocking:**
   • High storage costs
   • Space being taken up that could be used for other things
   • Money tied up in stock that could be used for other things

   Under stocking:
   • Potential to run out of stock
   • Organisation may get a bad reputation if it is unable to supply its customers
   • Low or no stock of raw materials may affect or halt production

   4

   (d) • Automatic updating of stock levels
   • Automatic ordering when stock reaches a certain level
   • Easy access to up-to-date information

   1

   Total marks 10

5. (a) Any 3 descriptions from:
   • Political
   • Environmental
   • Social
   • Technological
   • Economic
   • Competitive

   3

(b) • Good customer service promotes a positive image of the organisation
 • Happy customers will continue to use the organisation in the future
 • Good customer service encourages a good relationship to build between the customer and the organisation
 • The organisation develops a good reputation from continued good customer service

3

(c) • Ability of management
 • Available finance
 • Costs

2

(d) **Interest:**
 • Shareholders want the organisation to make a profit so that they can be paid a dividend

Influence:
 • Shareholders carry votes at the AGM and can influence the decision making

2

Total marks 10

6. (a) (i) • Newspaper
 • Internet
 • Company website
 • Job centre
 • Recruitment agency

2

(ii) **Advantages:**
 • Cheap (internet)
 • Wide distribution (website)
 • Expertise (agency)

Disadvantages:
 • Expensive (agency)
 • People may not know that vacancies are there unless they visit website

2

(b) • Represent employees in relation to pay, conditions of service, dismissal, redundancy, disagreement
 • Different trade unions for different types of employees
 • Carry out collective bargaining on behalf of their members
 • Can work at national or local level
 • Employers have a duty to engage with trade unions
 • Can place employees in a stronger position compared to acting on an individual basis

4

(c) • A legal requirement to keep employees safe while at work
 • Encourages safe working practices
 • Promotes the organisation as a responsible employer

2

Total marks 10

NATIONAL 5 BUSINESS MANAGEMENT MODEL PAPER 4

Se ction 1

1. (a) (i) Sole trader

1

 (ii) • From the case study — Gemma likes to offer a personal and tailored service to her customers to meet their needs
 • Providing extra assistance to a customer to ensure that their needs are completely satisfied

2

(b) **Costs:**
 • Web hosting
 • Website development and maintenance
 • Postage charges for sending out goods to customers

Benefits:
 • Increased market share
 • Ability to operate nationally/internationally
 • "Free" advertising

4

(c) • Advertising, e.g. radio, newspaper
 • Customer demonstrations
 • Free offers
 • Competitions
 • Discounts

3

(d) • Staff get better at their job
 • Increased motivation
 • It is easier to introduce changes
 • The image of the organisation is improved
 • Staff become more flexible

3

(e) • Rent
 • Electricity
 • Business rates
 • Advertising

2

Total marks 15

2. (a) (i) • Provide a service
 • Support learning
 • Be entrepreneurial

1

 (ii) • Products to use in learning
 • New ideas for teaching and learning
 • Ways to improve their business

2

(b) **Advantages:**
 • Available instantly
 • Little risk

Disadvantages:
 • Investor has a share in the business and how it is run
 • Share of profits needs to be paid to the investor

2

(c) **Advantages:**
 • Share the workload
 • Partners can specialise
 • Debts can be shared

Disadvantages:
 • There may be disagreements
 • Unlimited liability
 • Profits need to be shared

4

(d) • Horizontal integration
   • Vertical integration
   • Diversification

3

(e) **Advantages:**
   • Limited liability
   • Easier to raise finance
   • Better privacy of information compared to a plc

   Disadvantages:
   • Directors' legal duties
   • Public disclosure of information

3

Total marks 15

Section 2

3. (a) • Bank loan
   • Capital from partners
   • Retained profits

3

(b) • Essential for financial planning
   • Enables identification of cash surpluses and cash deficits
   • Avoid liquidity problems
   • Use information to secure additional finance, e.g. a bank

3

(c) • Reduce stock levels
   • Encourage debtors to pay quickly
   • Reduce cash outflows
   • Arrange a bank overdraft

2

(d) • Gross profit — profit from sales but before expenses
   • Net profit — gross profit minus business expenses

2

Total marks 10

4. (a) • Political
   • Economic
   • Social
   • Technological
   • Environmental
   • Competitive

4

(b) • Social responsibility — to meet the "green" agenda and have a social conscience in the eyes of customers
   • Profitability — businesses need to make a profit to meet the expectations of shareholders and owners and in order to survive
   • Survival — businesses need to survive in order to continue providing goods/services and make a profit

3

(c) • Have appropriate staff training in place
   • Have proper systems and processes in place to deal with customer complaints and enquiries
   • Seek feedback from customers
   • Employ dedicated staff to deal with customer services

3

Total marks 10

5. (a) • Introduction
   • Growth
   • Maturity

3

(b) • Special pricing
   • Special offers
   • Diversification
   • Improve the product
   • Rebrand

3

(c) • The market that the product will enter
   • The price of the competition
   • The desired profit to be made

2

(d) • Availability of distribution methods
   • Competition
   • Financial incentives

2

Total marks 10

6. (a) • Lost production
   • Loss of sales
   • Loss of customers
   • Negative image

2

(b) • Increased flexibility in workforce
   • Greater number of staff can lead to greater pool of experience
   • More adaptive to changing business needs
   • Ability to move staff around more easily increasing motivation

3

(c) • Use defined application and selection process
   • Testing – attainment, aptitude, psychometric, intelligence
   • Assessment centre
   • Interview process – one to one, panel, presentation

3

(d) • Need to have awareness of statutory responsibility in relation to race, age, gender, disability, faith, sexual orientation, etc.
   • Need to have an equal opportunities policy in place
   • Accurate record keeping required
   • Staff need to be trained to be aware of impact of legislation on the organisation and themselves
   • Encourage a safe and pleasant working environment for all staff

2

Total marks 10

NATIONAL 5 BUSINESS MANAGEMENT 2014

Questions that ask candidates to Describe . . .
Candidates must make a number of relevant, factual points up to the total mark allocation for the question. These should be key points. The points do not need to be in any particular order. Candidates may provide a number of straightforward points or a smaller number of developed points, or a combination of these.

Up to the total mark allocation for this question:
- 1 mark should be given for each accurate relevant point of knowledge.
- a second mark could be given for any point that is developed from the point of knowledge

Questions that ask candidates to Explain . . .
Candidates must make a number of points that relate cause and effect and/or make the relationships between things clear, for example by showing connections between a process/situation. These should be key reasons and may include theoretical concepts. There is no need to prioritise the reasons.

Candidates may provide a number of straightforward reasons or a smaller number of developed reasons, or a combination of these.

Up to the total mark allocation for this question:
- 1 mark should be given for each accurate relevant point of reason.
- a second mark could be given for any other point that is developed from the same reason

Questions that ask candidates to Compare . . .
Candidates must demonstrate a true comparison in order to gain any mark. Both sides of the point must be clear but need not be linked. Candidates can write several points regarding the first comparison item followed by several points on the second and the marker match the points using codes (eg a, b, c)

Up to the total mark allocation for this question:
- 1 mark should be given for each compared point

Section 1

1. (a) (i) Identifiable skills and qualities from the case study. Responses could include:
- Caroline has completed training
- Caroline has experience in managing a salon
- Caroline has experience in dog grooming
- Communication
- Planning eg business plan
- Decision making skills
- Financial skills
- Risk taking
- Creativity/come up with an idea

(ii) Responses could include:
- Training – can to provide her clients with a top quality service
- Managing a salon - able to manage the bookings and finance effectively
- Experienced in dog grooming - that she will be able to meet customer needs
  o Can train new staff to same high standard
- Communication skills – can build good relationships with customers or staff
  o Can make effective use of the business advisor

- Planning – can reduce the risk of failure
- Finance skills – so that she can avoid overspending

(b) Responses could include:
- A grant is money that does not need to be repaid whereas a loan is money that must be repaid
- With a grant no interest is incurred but with a loan interest will be added to the amount owed
- A grant is usually a one off payment whereas a loan can be requested several times
- Both types of finance from external sources

(c) Responses could include:
- Will ensure that customers return
  o This will increase the sales of the company
- Caroline will gain a good reputation
  o Which will entice new customers to try her business
- Caroline will be able to charge higher prices
- Customers will recommend to friends/family
- Caroline may receive less complaints from customers

(d) (i) Responses could include:
- Identify the vacancy
- Carry out a job analysis
- Create a job description
- Create a person specification
- Advertise the job
- Send out application forms

(ii) Responses could include:
- The Equality Act 2010 simplifies the current discrimination laws and puts them all together in one piece of legislation
- Any mention of the 9 protected characteristics
- Now includes workplace victimisation, harassment and bullying
- Prevents discrimination

(e) (i) Identifiable stage:
- Growth
- Maturity

(ii) Responses could include:
- Growth – customers awareness of the product increases/sales start to grow sharply
- Maturity – sales have reached their peak/she is fully booked up

2. (a) Identifiable objectives from the case study. Responses could include:
- The Big Issue has the objective to reduce homelessness whereas a public sector organisation has the objective to provide a service to a community
- Help homeless people earn a legitimate income whereas a public sector organisation has the objective to provide benefits for those in need
- Both the Big Issue and public sector organisations have the objective to make a difference
- The Big Issue has an objective to make a profit whereas a public sector organisation has the objective to use public funds effectively
- The Big Issue has an objective to increase awareness/sales whereas public sector organisation has the objective to provide a service
- Both organisations have the objective to be socially responsible

(b) (i) Identifiable method of promotion:
- Celebrity Endorsement/Celebrity Contributions

(ii) Responses could include:
- BOGOF – buy one get one free
- Free features – buy the product and get a complimentary product with it
- Discount for a limited time eg 25% extra
- Competitions – buy the product and enter a competition to win a prize
- Product endorsement...
- Fundraiser...
- TV advertising – producing audio-visual images to give information during commercial breaks
- Radio advertising – producing a radio advert sometimes with catchy tunes that can be played on local or national radio stations
- Newspaper/magazine advertising – images and information can be printed in local or national papers
- Outdoor media/billboards/transport – large images can be shown in prominent place/on the move
- Big Issue website – using their own website can give lots of information on their magazine and up and coming stories

(c) Responses could include:

Political
- Changes in laws may prevent the magazine from publishing certain stories
- Local councils may refuse to give vendors licences to sell on the streets

Economic
- There may be a reduction in consumer spending due to the recession
- Cost of producing the magazine may increase due to inflation

Social
- There may be greater sympathy to homelessness which could increase sales of The Big Issue

Technological
- The growth in electronic newsstands/apps may lead to a decrease in demand for paper magazines

Environmental
- The weather eg heavy snow may prevent vendors from being able to go to their pitch to sell The Big Issue
- Road works may mean delivery of the magazine is late in arriving from the distribution points

Competition
- Competition from other magazines may mean that The Big Issue loses sales
- Other charity organisations do street/shop donations may take money away from Big Issue vendors

(d) (i) Responses could include:
- Air – plane
- Road – van, lorry, car
- Sea – boat
- Pipeline
- Electronic

(ii) Responses could include:
- **Air**
  o Provides fast transportation worldwide
  o Can be affected by weather/delays
  o Is relatively expensive
  o Not direct – another mode of transport is required when the delivery reaches the airport
- **Road**
  o Allows door-to-door delivery
  o Can depart at any time/24 hours
  o Restrictions to the number of hours a lorry driver can work
  o Petrol prices increases makes this more expensive
- **Sea**
  o It is more environmentally friendly
  o Can handle bulky goods
  o Goods may require additional road haulage to arrive at final destination
  o Slower method of transportation than others
- Pipeline...
- Electronic...

(e) Responses could include:
- Profit to be made
- Cost of production
  o These may include materials and labour costs
- Price of other magazines/competitors
- Image to be generated
  o More up-market image may mean a higher price is charged
- Income to be provided to vendors
- Target market
- What customers are willing to pay
- Break-even point
- Demand ...

Section 2

3. (a) Responses could include:

Advantages
- Item can be reused to make new products
- Takes less energy to recycle than to extract new materials
- Limits the items ending up in landfills
  o Reduces cost of landfills as less are required
  o Improves the image of an organisation
- May be cheaper to produce using recycled materials
- Can give a competitive edge

Disadvantages
- Need to be sorted into different categories which takes time to do
- Some items can only be recycled a limited amount of times ie paper
- May be seen as inferior
- May reduce quality

(b) Responses could include:
- Money tied up in stock which could be used to improve another area
- Goods may deteriorate which could lead to high wastage costs
- Greater chance of theft which could mean loss of profit from unsold goods
- Greater storage/insurance costs which could mean prices may need to rise

- Goods may become obsolete - this wastes money as no-one is willing to buy

(c) (i) Responses could include:
- Quality Circles
- Benchmarking
- Quality Assurance
- Total Quality Management
- Quality Control
- Quality Standards
- Quality Inputs **(each separate)**
  Quality raw materials; training of staff; maintenance of machinery/equipment

(ii) Responses could include:

Quality Circles
- Small group of employees who meet regularly to discuss how to improve methods of working

Benchmarking
- Trying to match the standard of the quality leader/competitor

Quality Assurance
- To ensure 'right first time' and prevent errors
- Checking at every stage of the production process

Total Quality Management
- Continuous process where each employee takes responsibility to ensure quality is consistent with every product

Quality Control
- Checks at the beginning and end of the production process only

Quality Standards
- When the product reaches the required standard it can be awarded a quality logo
- Give customers confidence

Quality Inputs – each separate
- Raw materials need to be of quality in order to obtain a quality final product
- All staff must be trained so they are competent and are all working to the same quality standards
- Machines need to be maintained so that they do not make mistakes affecting quality

4. (a) Responses could include:
- Fixed Costs – costs which do not vary with output or sales
- Variable Costs – costs which do vary with output or sales
- Sales Revenue – the income received from sale of goods/services

(b) Responses could include:
- Change to cheaper supplier/new supplier
  o Look to see if you can get bulk buying discount
- Reduce wages
  o Cut overtime
  o Release temporary staff
- Reduce utilities usage
  o Move to energy saving light bulbs
  o Fit sensors to switch lights off after a period of time of no motion
- Reduce advertising/switch to cheaper methods
  o Set up own website
  o Send adverts through e-mail
  o Advertise in newspapers rather than on TV
- Move to cheaper premises to reduce rent

- Improve budgeting
- Use machinery instead of employees (automation)
- Hire purchase/leasing to spread payments

(c) (i) Responses could include:
- Formulae can be used to calculate information
  o Allows for automatic calculation if anything changes
  o Reduces error
- Information can be saved and edited later
- Templates can be used for financial information – eg Cash Budgets/Profit Statements
  o Standardisation of documents means that processes are easily replicated
- Graphs/Charts can be created to display information
  o Allows easier comparison of difficult financial information

(ii) Responses could include:
- Word Processing – to create documents informing departments of their annual budget figure
- Word Processing – to compile the Shareholders' Annual Financial Report
- Database – to keep records of suppliers' accounts due and/or debtors' accounts owed
- Database – to create reports of overdue accounts
- PowerPoint – to display financial information at the shareholders meeting
- Internet/website/online...

5. (a) Responses could include:
- Collect CVs/application forms
- Creating a short list/leet of suitable applicants
  o Compare the application forms to the job and person specification
  o Seek references from previous employers
- Interviews on a one-to-one or panel basis
  o Asking each potential employee a series of questions to allow for comparison
- Testing to provide additional information as to a candidate's suitability
  o Attainment – demonstrates skills
  o Aptitude – natural abilities
  o Intelligence – mental ability
- Successful candidate(s) informed/make the final choice
- Unsuccessful candidate(s) informed

(b) (i) Responses may include:
- **Sit in** – employees remain in the workplace but do not work
- **Overtime ban** – employees refuse to work overtime
- **Work to rule** – employees only undertake tasks stated in their job description
- **Go slow** – employees produce work at a slower rate
- **Strike** – last resort, where employees withdraw labour/refuse to work
  o Often accompanied by demonstrations, marches and a picket line
- **Withdrawal of overtime** – employer removes the opportunity for employees to work overtime
- **Lock out** – employees are locked out of the business premises
- **Close** – last resort action where a factory or workplace is closed and relocated
- **Boycott...**

(ii) Responses could include:
- Production within the organisation may come to a halt therefore the organisation could struggle to produce goods to meet customer demand
  - o Causing customers to go elsewhere
  - o Could damage the reputation of the organisation
- Delays in the production of goods can lead to loss of sales revenue as customers cancel orders
- Employees refusing to work overtime or going slow would slow down production
  - o Creating a poor image or reputation
- Company's share price may fall due to the poor reputation of the firm
- Organisation may find it difficult to recruit staff as they have a poor image with potential employees

(c) Responses could include:
- Piece-rate is where they are paid by the units produced (or sales made) whereas time-rate is where employees are paid by the hour
- Piece-rate means the more units produced, the higher the pay whereas time-rate means the more hours worked the higher the pay
- Piece-rate means quality may suffer in order to get quantity whereas time-rate pay may result in a higher standard of output
- Piece-rate is often used for unskilled/factory workers whereas time-rate pay is used for skilled workers (could be flipped)

6. (a) Responses could include:
- Availability of finance
- Availability of staff
- Availability of time
- Experience/Training of staff
- Equipment available
- Current technology
- Quality of products
- Leadership/Quality of management

(b) Responses could include:
- **Land** – this refers to all natural resources
  - o This includes farmland, water and coal
  - o The reward for land is rent
- **Labour** – this is the workforce (employees)
  - o The reward for labour is wages
- **Capital** – these are man-made resources
  - o This includes premises, equipment, machinery
  - o The money invested in the organisation
  - o The reward for capital is interest
- **Enterprise** – the idea for the business
  - o The person who brings together the other 3 factors of production
  - o The reward for enterprise is profit

(c) (i) Responses could include:
- Owners/Shareholders
- Employees
- Managers
- Suppliers
- Lenders/Creditors
- Government
- Local Community
- Customers
- Pressure Groups

(ii) Responses could include:

Owners
- Make major decisions which can lead to mistakes being made resulting in less profit
- Can vary their level of investment which will impact the decision the organisation can make

Employees
- Can vary the quality of the work they produce which may result in wastage or complaints
- Can carry out industrial action which will impact on the amount being produced

Suppliers
- Can vary the quality of their supplies which affects the quality of final product
- Can delay delivery which will halt production

Lenders/Creditors
- Can vary the level of interest applied to loans which could make them more affordable
- Set the time frame for repayment which will affect the cash outflows every month

Government
- Can change legislation which may cost the organisation more money to implement
- Can change council policies/restrictions which make it easier for the organisation to gain planning permission

Local community
- Can protest about the actions of an organisation which can influence their image

Customers
- Can take their custom elsewhere which influences the organisation's level of sales

Pressure Groups
- Can protest against the organisation's decisions/policies causing questions to be raised by the public

Acknowledgements

Permission has been sought from all relevant copyright holders and Hodder Gibson is grateful for the use of the following:

An extract adapted from http://www.psybt.org.uk/case-study/palladium-executive-hire (December 2012) © The Prince's Scottish Youth Business Trust (SQP page 2);

A photograph of Asif Ali © Palladium Executive Hire (SQP page 2);

An extract © SEC Ltd (SQP page 3);

A photograph © Foster + Partners (SQP page 3);

An extract from http://roadwisedrivertraining.co.uk © Aberdeen Foyer (Model Paper 1 page 2);

The logos for Aberdeen Foyer and Roadwise Driver Training © Aberdeen Foyer (Model Paper 1 page 2);

An extract and logo from http://www.angussoftfruits.co.uk © Angus Soft Fruits Ltd (Model Paper 1 page 3);

An extract from http://www.xtremesolutionsltd.com © Xtreme Business Solutions Ltd (Model Paper 2 page 2);

An extract adapted from http://www.bbc.co.uk/news/uk-scotland-north-east-orkney-shetland-22018373 (4th April 2013) © BBC News (Model Paper 2 page 3);

An extract and logo from http://www.the-chocolate-tree.co.uk © The Chocolate Tree (Model Paper 3 page 2);

An extract and logo from http://www.traid.org.uk © TRAID (Model Paper 3 page 3);

An extract and logo from http://www.justdogsshop.co.uk © Just Dogs (Model Paper 4 page 2);

An extract and logo from http://www.treeof.com © TOK (Scotland) Ltd (Model Paper 4 page 3);

An image and text for Dogs Body Design, taken from 'The Southern Reporter' 22 February 2013 © Johnston Press PLC (2014 page 2);

The cover of The Big Issue magazine from February 20-26, 2012 (No 988) © The Big Issue Foundation (2014 page 3).

An article adapted from http://www.bigissue.com/about-us and http://www.socialenterprise.org.uk/about/about-social-enterprise/FAQs/test-case-study/case-studies/big-issue © The Big Issue Foundation & Social Enterprise (2014 page 3).

Hodder Gibson would like to thank SQA for use of any past exam questions that may have been used in model papers, whether amended or in original form.